E PICTURE BOOK MON

Moncure, Jane Belk.

Word Bird's Thanksgiving
words

Word Bird's Thanksgiving Words

E
PICTURE
BOOK
MON

Published in the United States of America by The Child's World®, Inc.
PO Box 326
Chanhassen, MN 55317-0326
800-599-READ
www.childsworld.com

Project Manager Mary Berendes
Editor Katherine Stevenson, Ph.D.
Designer Ian Butterworth

Library of Congress Cataloging-in-Publication Data
Moncure, Jane Belk.
Word Bird's Thanksgiving words / by Jane Belk Moncure.
p. cm.
Summary: Word Bird puts words about Thanksgiving in his word house—
Pilgrims, Indian corn, pumpkin pie, and others.
ISBN 1-56766-628-0 (lib. bdg. : alk. paper)
1. Vocabulary—Juvenile literature. 2. Thanksgiving Day—Juvenile literature.
[1. Vocabulary. 2. Thanksgiving Day. 3. Holidays.]   I.Title.
PE1449 .M5335 2001
428.1—dc21
00-010886

Word Bird's

Thanksgiving Words

by Jane Belk Moncure

illustrated by Chris McEwan

Word Bird made a...

word house.

"I will put Thanksgiving
words in my house,"
said Word Bird.

Word Bird put in
these words:

Mayflower

Plymouth Rock

8

Pilgrims

Native Americans

Native American homes

Indian corn

harvest

the first
Thanksgiving

Pilgrim hats

Pilgrim ship

Native American headdress

teepee

Native American foods

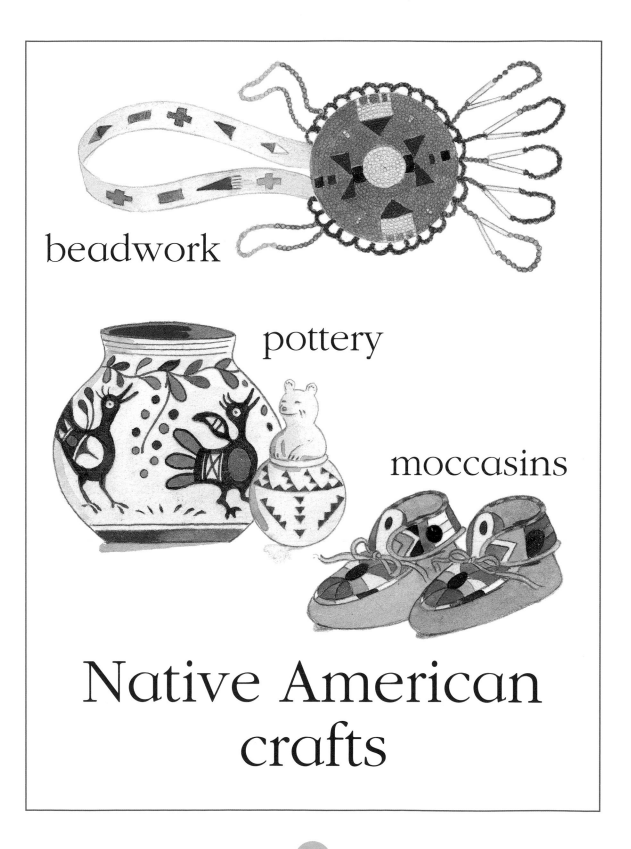

beadwork

pottery

moccasins

Native American crafts

Native American drums

Native American dance

Thanksgiving
basket

turkey

pumpkin pie

Thanksgiving
dinner

friends

family

giving thanks

Can you read these Thanksgiving

Mayflower

harvest

Plymouth Rock

the first Thanksgiving

Native Americans

Pilgrim hats

Native American homes

Native American headdress

Indian corn

teepee

words with Word Bird?

Native American foods

Thanksgiving basket

Native American crafts

turkey

Native American drums

pumpkin pie

Native American dance

giving thanks

You can make a Thanksgiving word house. You can put Word Bird's words in your house and read them, too.

Pilgrim

pumpkin pie

turkey

Can you think of other Thanksgiving words to put in your word house?